THE NHL: HISTORY AND HEROES

MINNESOTA WILD

LISA M. BOLT SIMONS

THE NHL: HISTORY AND HEROES

Published by Creative Education
P.O. Box 227, Mankato, Minnesota 56002
Creative Education is an imprint of The Creative Company.

DESIGN AND PRODUCTION BY **ZENO DESIGN**

Printed in the United States of America

PHOTOGRAPHS BY Getty Images (Allsport/Allsport, Brian Bahr/NHLI, Bruce
Bennett Studios, Jonathan Daniel, Elsa, Jeff Gross, Bruce Kluckhohn, Robert
Laberge, Ron LeBlanc, Len Redkoles, Ryan/Beyer, Jamie Sabau/NHLI, Scott A.
Schneider, Don Smith, Jeff Vinnick/NHLI)

LIBRARY OF CONGRESS CATALOGING-IN-PUBLICATION DATA

Simons, Lisa M. B., 1969–
The story of the Minnesota Wild / by Lisa M. Bolt Simons.
p. cm. — (The NHL: history and heroes)
Includes index.
ISBN 978-1-58341-685-3
1. Minnesota Wild (Hockey team) 2. Hockey teams—Minnesota—Saint Paul.
3. Hockey—United States. I. Title. II. Series.

GV848.M58S56 2008
796.962'6409776579—dc22   2008000092

First Edition

9 8 7 6 5 4 3 2 1

COVER: Wing Marian Gaborik

CREATIVE ⚫ EDUCATION

MINNESOTA

WILD

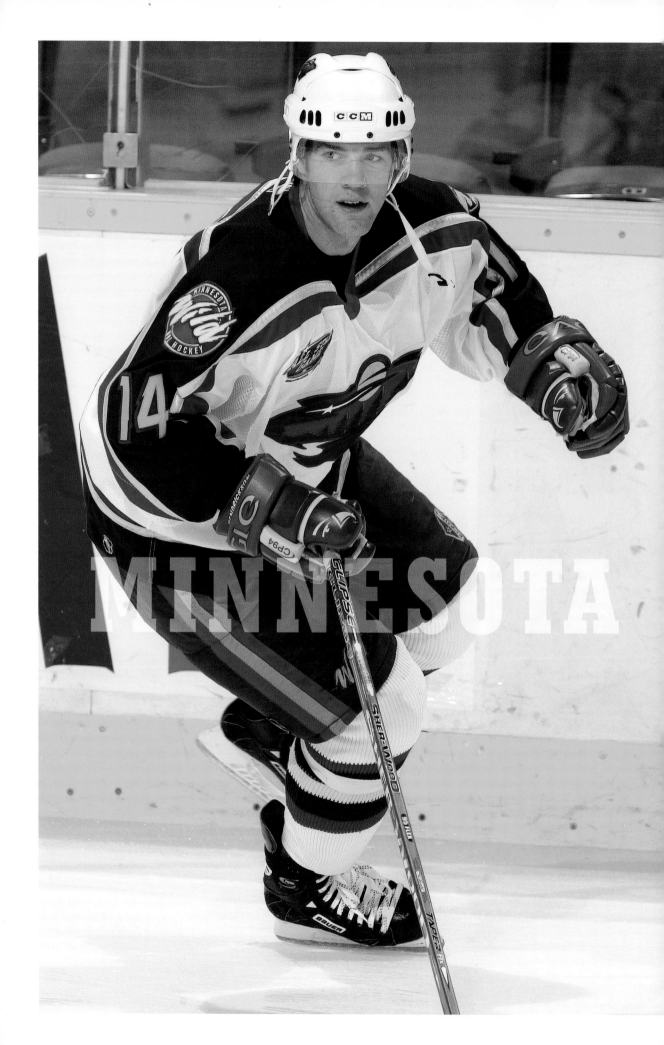

ON OCTOBER 11, 2000, BEFORE A CROWD OF 18,827 FANS DRESSED IN RED AND GREEN, UNIVERSITY OF MINNESOTA HOCKEY LEGEND JOHN MAYASICH ANNOUNCED, "IN THE STATE OF HOCKEY, WE SKATE THE FROZEN PONDS. WE LIVE THE GAME. WELCOME TO MINNESOTA...." ST. PAUL MAYOR NORM COLEMAN THEN DROPPED A CEREMONIAL PUCK ONTO THE ICE, MOMENTS BEFORE THE REAL PUCK WAS DROPPED. PHILADELPHIA FLYERS CENTER KENT MANDERVILLE WON THE FACE-OFF, BUT MINNESOTA CENTER DARBY HENDRICKSON SOON NETTED A FIRST-PERIOD GOAL, DRAWING A ROAR FROM THE FANS. THE CROWD HAD PILED INTO

THE NEW XCEL ENERGY CENTER IN DOWNTOWN ST. PAUL TO WATCH THE WILD, AN EXPANSION NATIONAL HOCKEY LEAGUE FRANCHISE, PLAY ITS FIRST REGULAR-SEASON HOME GAME. AND ALTHOUGH THE GAME'S OUTCOME, A 3–3 TIE, WAS NOT QUITE WHAT THE HOME CROWD WAS HOPING FOR, IN MANY WAYS IT WAS A HUGE VICTORY. AFTER A SEVEN-YEAR ABSENCE, PRO HOCKEY WAS BACK IN MINNESOTA.

BORN TO
BE WILD

MINNESOTA IS FAR ENOUGH NORTH THAT
one border touches Canada. The state's business
and cultural center is the "Twin Cities" area of St.
Paul, its capital, and Minneapolis, its most populous
city. The Mississippi River—which divides the Twin
Cities, "The Land of 10,000 Lakes," and the United
States itself—begins in Itasca State Park in northern
Minnesota. The name "Minnesota" comes from the
Dakota Indian language and means "sky-tinted
water." Sometimes as early as October, that water
freezes as snow and ice descend on the land, turn-
ing lakes, ponds, and rivers into skating rinks. With
such an abundance of frozen water, Minnesota is
the perfect setting for hockey.

St. Paul is a city that celebrates winter, famous for its knowledgeable hockey fans and its annual Winter Carnival, complete with ice sculpting.

Starting in 1967, Minnesota was represented in the National Hockey League (NHL) by a team called the North Stars. The team built a loyal following and enjoyed its share of success, but in 1993, team owner Norm Green—citing discontent with the team's arena situation—broke the hearts of Minnesota hockey fans by moving the franchise to Dallas, Texas. But the outlook was not entirely grim. Even before the Zamboni machine had finished cleaning the ice at the Metropolitan Sports Center after the North Stars' last home game in April 1993, numerous organizations and individuals, including Minnesota governor Arne Carlson and investor Robert Naegele Jr., were hatching plans to bring big-time hockey back to the Twin Cities. The Metropolitan Sports Facilities Commission, a group that owned the "Met" Center, budgeted money to help find another NHL team.

In the mid-1990s, St. Paul mayor Norm Coleman helped lead attempts to attract one of several existing NHL teams, including the Winnipeg Jets, to

Wes Walz CENTER

Walz first laced his hockey skates at age six and began his NHL career with the Boston Bruins 13 years later. He spent time playing in Switzerland, Philadelphia, Calgary, and Detroit as well before joining the new Wild franchise. A valuable leader, tireless skater, and tough checker with a knack for killing penalties, Walz had a work ethic that kept him fit even in his late 30s. "You look at him train, and the young guys can't train as much as he does," said Wild coach Jacques Lemaire. "They can't do what he does." Walz retired from the NHL in 2007.

WILD SEASONS: 2000–07
HEIGHT: 5-11
WEIGHT: 190

• 607 career NHL games
• Wild-record 14 short-handed goals
• 2003 Selke Trophy finalist (as best defensive forward)
• career-high 27 assists in 1993–94

The North Stars, led by such players as center Mike Modano, captivated Minnesota in 1991 with a stunning playoff run to the Stanley Cup Finals.

Minnesota. But despite the Commission's money and Coleman's recruiting efforts, no team came. The city of St. Paul tried another route two years later by applying to the NHL for a new expansion team. "If we miss this opportunity, it will be like the comet Kohoutek," St. Paul city council member Dan Bostrom said. "It won't be back around for another 1,000 years."

Finally, on June 25, 1997, hopeful Minnesotans received the news for which they had been waiting. The NHL's Board of Governors announced that four new expansion teams—including one in St. Paul—would be added to the league, with Minnesota's beginning play in the year 2000. After the announcement, work quickly began on a proper home for the new team. Construction crews demolished the St. Paul Civic Center Arena, a 25-year-old building in downtown St. Paul, to make way for a new arena.

As the demolition proceeded, a team management staff that included executive Jac Sperling considered a team name after receiving some 13,000 suggestions from fans. The Minnesota Blue Ox, Freeze, Northern Lights, White Bears, and Voyageurs were all popular choices, but on January 22, 1998, the new NHL team was named the Minnesota Wild. "We think it represents what Minnesota hockey fans hold most dear—our rugged natural wilderness, the premier brand of hockey that's native to Minnesota, and the great enthusiasm of all our hockey fans," said Sperling. When the Wild home sweater was unveiled in November 1999, it featured an animal that had the North Star for an eye, evergreen trees and red for fur, a sun or moon for an ear, and a stream for a mouth. The bearish creature appeared to be growling.

Goodbye Met, Hello Xcel

BEFORE THE HUGE GLASS FACADE OF the Xcel Energy Center, home of the Wild, could sparkle on the corner of 7th Street and Kellogg in downtown St. Paul, the old Civic Center, a multipurpose building used to host lower-level hockey games and other events, had to be destroyed. But it was the demise of the Metropolitan Sports Center in Bloomington, a suburb 20 miles away, that truly tore out the hearts of many hockey fans, as it had been the home of the Minnesota North Stars for 26 years. The Met Center came to an end on a bitterly cold December 13, 1994.

That day, teenager Michael Franson, a hockey fan who suffered from a blood disorder and who had been given season tickets to the University of Minnesota home hockey games by the Make-A-Wish Foundation, pushed a button that sent a charge through wires connected to 579 explosives planted within the Met Center. The blast leveled most of the structure, and bulldozers razed the portions that remained standing. To many fans, it was a symbolic and bittersweet transition—the story of the North Stars had ended, and the story of the Wild was about to begin.

THE RETURN
OF HOCKEY

IN MAY 2000, THE WILD BEGAN BUILDING
their first roster by signing wing Steve Aronson, a
player from the small University of St. Thomas in St.
Paul. During the NHL Entry Draft in June, the Wild
used the third overall pick to select 18-year-old
Marian Gaborik, an exceptionally speedy center from
Slovakia. The team also obtained a number of players
through free-agent signings and a special Expansion
Draft. Among those players were center Wes Walz,
a crafty veteran of six NHL seasons; center Darby
Hendrickson, a Minnesota native; defensemen Filip
Kuba and Brad Bombardir, both of whom arrived
with NHL playoff experience; and aggressive goalie

Although he was a rarely used backup during his five seasons in Dallas, Manny Fernandez quickly earned acclaim as Minnesota's starting goalie.

Manny Fernandez, who was acquired from the Dallas Stars. As these players prepared for training camp, construction crews put the finishing touches on the club's new arena, which was to be named the Xcel Energy Center.

On June 19, 2000, amid the player additions, Wild general manager Doug Risebrough introduced Jacques Lemaire as the head coach of the new franchise. Risebrough and Lemaire knew each other well, having played as teammates for the Montreal Canadiens in the 1970s. Lemaire, a stern leader with a thick French-Canadian accent, had previously coached the New Jersey Devils, leading them to a Stanley Cup championship in 1995. He preached a philosophy that involved tight defense and kept games low-scoring—a so-called "trapping" style that irritated some hockey purists but that Wild management thought would be perfect for a new team with limited talent.

The Wild made their NHL debut on October 11, tying the Philadelphia

WILD ALL-TIME TEAM

Marian Gaborik WING

Gaborik, who was born on Valentine's Day 1982 in Trencin, Czechoslovakia (now Slovakia), began setting Minnesota records after the Wild selected him with the third overall pick in the 2000 NHL Draft. He scored the first goal in the Wild's first regular-season game at the tender age of 18 years, 7 months, and 20 days. Gaborik was recognized as one of the swiftest skaters in the game, and his passion for speed extended off the ice, where he took an interest in car racing. In 2005, he opened MG Arena in his hometown to offer local kids more ice time.

WILD SEASONS: 2000–present
HEIGHT: 6-1
WEIGHT: 199

- 196 career goals
- 4th player in NHL history with five hat tricks (at least three goals in one game) before age 21
- member of the 2006 Slovakian Olympic team
- 2-time All-Star

Wes Walz assembled a well-traveled pro career—playing for four different NHL clubs as well as a Swiss team—before taking the ice for the Wild.

Flyers. Although they proceeded to lose a lot of games that season, they played respectable hockey as they notched various team "firsts." The Wild earned their first victory on October 18 against the Tampa Bay Lightning. On November 24, Fernandez stopped all 27 shots by the Chicago Blackhawks, securing Minnesota's first shutout victory. Two days later, winger Antti Laaksonen used his nimble moves to post the franchise's first hat trick (three goals in one game) in a home game against the Vancouver Canucks.

Wild fans enjoyed every scrappy effort, but they savored two victories in particular that first season. When the Dallas Stars returned to Minnesota in December, the Wild netted six goals, including three by Minnesota natives—two by Hendrickson and one by wing Jeff Nielsen—in a 6–0 drubbing. "It felt like a playoff game," Nielsen said. "You could feel the electricity in the air." In February, the Wild beat the Stars again, this time 2–1 in Texas. Minnesota went on to finish the season with a 25–39–18 record.

"It's obvious we never should've left."

NHL COMMISSIONER GARY BETTMAN
AT THE WILD'S FIRST HOME GAME IN 2000

The Wild started their second season with a bang. Amazingly, after the first six games, they were the only undefeated team in the NHL. And even though the rest of the season again featured more losses than wins, the Wild continued to improve. Defenseman Willie Mitchell emerged as a formidable presence, combining speed with size to lock down opponents. Defenseman Nick Schultz made his NHL debut in October, and a month later, high-energy

Split Rock in St. Paul

IN 1997, WHEN MARK ANGER LEARNED that St. Paul would be building a new hockey arena, he applied for the job. A longtime hockey fan and registered architect of 19 years, Anger was finishing up the BankAtlantic Center for the Florida Panthers NHL team at the time and saw the Minnesota project as an opportunity to come home. After getting the project, Anger said that the design team "had a branding theme for the arena, that of the outdoors, from the prairies of southern Minnesota to the northern woods." One morning, as Anger looked at the half-finished elevator shaft being constructed at Gate 1, he had the idea to place stone around it to resemble a lighthouse tower. Inside the arena, Anger wanted another lighthouse. Thinking of the Split Rock Lighthouse in northern Minnesota on a cliff above Lake Superior, Anger knew the perfect location for such a structure inside the arena—on a platform around the northwest corner column, high above the ice. Today, during any Xcel Energy Center event, a light spins in the lantern gallery on top of the tower outside Gate 1. During Wild games, whenever the home team scores, a horn blasts and a light spins in the northwest corner "lighthouse" in celebration.

wing Richard Park skated in a Wild sweater for the first time. These players helped Minnesota earn one of its biggest victories yet in November, as the Wild took down the defending Stanley Cup champion Colorado Avalanche 4–2.

Minnesota faded late in the season to end up 26–35–21, but the fans that filled Xcel Energy Center for every game saw hope beyond the losses. Gaborik was a rapidly rising star who netted 30 goals on the season, Andrew Brunette was a versatile wing who paced the offense with a career-high 48 assists, and such players as centers Jim Dowd and Sergei Zholtok had proven their mettle. And Coach Lemaire's defensive style seemed to be working, as the Wild were competitive even in many of their defeats.

"Defense comes from discipline. It binds players to do the same things. It creates a camaraderie because they all have to do it."

MINNESOTA GENERAL MANAGER DOUG RISEBROUGH

18

WILD

Just the second Korean-born NHL player ever, Richard Park notched at least 24 points (goals plus assists) in each of his three Wild seasons.

THE COMEBACK PLAYOFFS

THE WILD'S THIRD CAMPAIGN PROVED TO BE their breakthrough season. They beat the Boston Bruins 5–1 in the season opener and then kept rolling, building up an 8–1–2 record. In January, the team sent its first player to the annual NHL All-Star Game, as Gaborik suited up for the Western Conference and won the weekend's "Fastest Skater" competition. Thanks largely to superb play by the goalie duo of Fernandez and Dwayne Roloson, Minnesota went on to finish the season with 42 wins and earn its first NHL playoff berth.

Goalie Dwayne Roloson, a key to the Wild's 2003 playoff run, was a late bloomer, not making his first All-Star Game until the age of 34.

As the sixth of eight playoff seeds in the Western Conference, the Wild met a powerful first-round opponent: the heavily favored Colorado Avalanche. The Wild continued their surprising play by upsetting Colorado 4–2 in Game 1, but the series seemed to return to script as the Avs beat the Wild the next three games. Minnesota, though, refused to fold. It stayed alive with a 3–2 win in Game 5, then thrilled the Xcel crowd by pulling out an overtime win in Game 6. Richard Park sent the crowd into a frenzy as he took a pass from Wes Walz and zipped the puck between the legs of star goaltender Patrick Roy.

The deciding Game 7 was in Denver, and the Wild and Avs skated to a 2–2 knot by the end of regulation. Then, barely three minutes into the extra period, Brunette corralled the puck and attacked the Colorado goal. After weaving through defenders, Brunette deftly wrapped the puck around Roy's left skate and flipped it into the net, making the Pepsi Center go silent except for

Andrew Brunette WING

Brunette seemed to like being one of the new guys. After scoring the Nashville Predators' first goal during their inaugural 1998–99 season, Brunette played two years for the expansion Atlanta Thrashers. He then signed with Minnesota during the Wild's second season and stayed until 2004. Brunette's greatest Minnesota moment came when he scored the game-winning, overtime goal against Colorado Avalanche goaltender Patrick Roy in Game 7 of the 2003 Western Conference quarterfinals. Coach Jacques Lemaire said that the dependable and relentless "Bruno" was "extremely talented, probably the most talented around the net who played for us in all these years."

WILD SEASONS: 2001–04
HEIGHT: 6-1
WEIGHT: 210

- 183 career goals
- 344 career assists
- played in 430 consecutive games from January 2002 through February 2008
- 11 career playoff goals

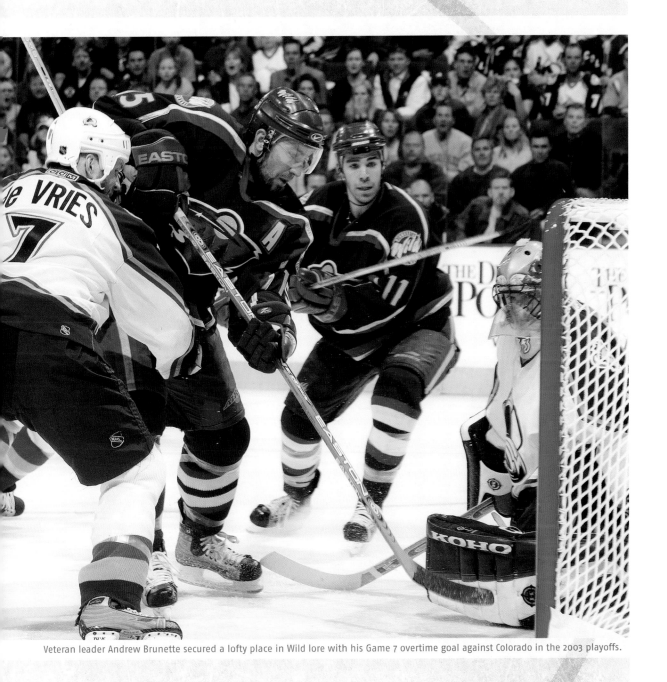

Veteran leader Andrew Brunette secured a lofty place in Wild lore with his Game 7 overtime goal against Colorado in the 2003 playoffs.

23

the celebration of the Wild players. The goal was the last that the great Roy would surrender in his Hall of Fame career, as he retired after the loss. "It's kind of a blur," said Brunette. "You can't believe it happened."

After pulling off one of the greatest upsets in recent NHL postseason history, the Wild assumed the role of underdog again as they faced the Vancouver Canucks in the next round. The two Northwest Division opponents came into the series with a heated rivalry, and after the Wild won Game 2 in Vancouver to tie the series, a brawl erupted between the teams. The bad blood continued in Minnesota in Game 3, as brawny Wild winger Matt Johnson and Canucks wing Brad May exchanged punches just seven seconds after the face-off. Vancouver won that game and the next to put Minnesota on the brink of elimination. But once again, Coach Lemaire's team would not quit. After the Wild crushed the Canucks 7–2 in Game 5, Minnesota sportswriter Patrick Reusse noted, "If the Canucks react as did Colorado, blaming Game 5 on a poor effort rather than a tough, smart, talented opponent, they are headed for the same fate … and these Wild players are headed for comeback immortality."

After the Wild again dominated Game 6, winning 5–1 at home, the teams flew back to Vancouver for a deciding Game 7. The game was tied at 2–2 with six minutes left before Hendrickson put the Wild ahead with a hard slap shot. Minutes later, wing Pascal Dupuis sealed Minnesota's victory by batting a deflected puck past Canucks goalie Dan Cloutier. Against all odds, the Wild had overcome a second straight three-games-to-one deficit, a feat never before accomplished in the long history of the NHL. Minnesota had indeed attained comeback immortality.

Hockey Conservation

Sergei Zholtok

THE MINNESOTA WILD ARE THE ONLY NHL franchise with a team curator, or historian, on its staff. Since February 2000, Roger Godin has been responsible for maintaining and updating hockey exhibits in the Xcel Energy Center. Godin was the first U.S. Hockey Hall of Fame executive director in Eveleth, Minnesota, when it opened in 1973. The Xcel exhibits, which include various artifacts, headlines, and photographs, relate to hockey throughout Minnesota, "which is unlike most other places in the United States," Godin said. "We have a history and a culture behind it that extends back to the 1890s." The exhibits cover all levels of competitive hockey, both amateur and professional. College player awards are located on the lower concourse, boys' and girls' high school jerseys are framed on the suite level, and a historic player (names are changed periodically) is featured in the Hockey Lodge team store. The Wild franchise is honored with a display of its first season in the lower corridor, a banner proclaiming the 2003 playoff run hanging from the ceiling by the arena's north glass wall, and a memorial to former Wild center Sergei Zholtok, who died in November 2004 during a game in his native Latvia.

That was as far as the Wild would go, however. They took on the Mighty Ducks of Anaheim in the Western Conference Finals but ran into red-hot goalie Jean-Sebastien Giguere, who turned away every one of Minnesota's shots in the first three games. In Game 4, Brunette finally slipped a goal past Giguere's pads on an assist from center Cliff Ronning, but it wasn't enough. The Ducks beat the Wild 2-1 to sweep the series. Still, Coach Lemaire could not have been prouder of his team. "We went in the playoffs," he said, "and we were not supposed to win one game."

"We still don't know what that animal is on the front of the Wild sweater, but we are now certain of this: It's something that can't be killed."

MINNESOTA SPORTSWRITER PATRICK REUSSE
DURING THE WILD'S 2003 PLAYOFF RUN

26

WILD

Center Cliff Ronning spent only one season in a Wild sweater, but he came up big during the 2003 playoffs, posting two goals and seven assists.

BACK TO REALITY

AFTER THEIR PHENOMENAL PLAYOFF RIDE, the Wild were hoping for more of the same in 2003–04. Most of the players responsible for the team's magical run were back, including Gaborik, Brunette, Park, and the goalie tandem of Fernandez and Roloson. After adding such players as rookie defenseman Brent Burns, Minnesota won its home opener and then ended a mediocre stretch by assembling a nine-game unbeaten streak in December. The Wild also made franchise history by netting eight goals in an 8–2 blowout win over Chicago in March.

Even as a rookie, 6-foot-4 defenseman and fan favorite Brent Burns showed star potential, combining size and speed with a hard slap shot.

Although the Wild just missed the playoffs with a 30–29–23 record, there were a number of individual highlights worth celebrating. Roloson, a goalie who seemed to thrive in clutch situations, won the Roger Crozier Saving Grace Award, given to the goaltender with the NHL's best save percentage. He and Kuba, a defenseman known for his speed and tireless effort, were named to the 2004 All-Star team. The All-Star weekend afforded Minnesota the chance to show off its hockey pride and its beautiful Xcel Energy Center, as St. Paul played host to the midseason festivities.

The Xcel, and hockey arenas throughout America and Canada, went silent in 2004–05, as the entire season was cancelled due to a salary dispute between NHL owners and players. After the issue was finally resolved in July 2005, many hockey fans were soured by the experience, and attendance fell league-wide. In Minnesota, however, the enthusiasm remained high, and

Willie Mitchell DEFENSEMAN

Mitchell figure skated when he was young and discovered he was good at going backwards. As a hockey player in his teens, he switched from forward to defenseman, where his knack for skating in reverse would be useful. Nicknamed "Bill Pickle" by wing Andrew Brunette (a reference to his favorite snack), Mitchell earned a reputation as both a tough and intelligent defender after being traded to Minnesota from the New Jersey Devils. Wild fans loved him, and opponents respected him. As Vancouver Canucks head coach Alain Vigneault said, "Give Willie Mitchell a tough assignment, and he'll treat it like life and death."

WILD SEASONS: 2000–06
HEIGHT: 6-3
WEIGHT: 205

- 508 career penalty minutes
- 68 career assists
- team captain in December 2005
- 4 career playoff assists

WILD ALL-TIME TEAM

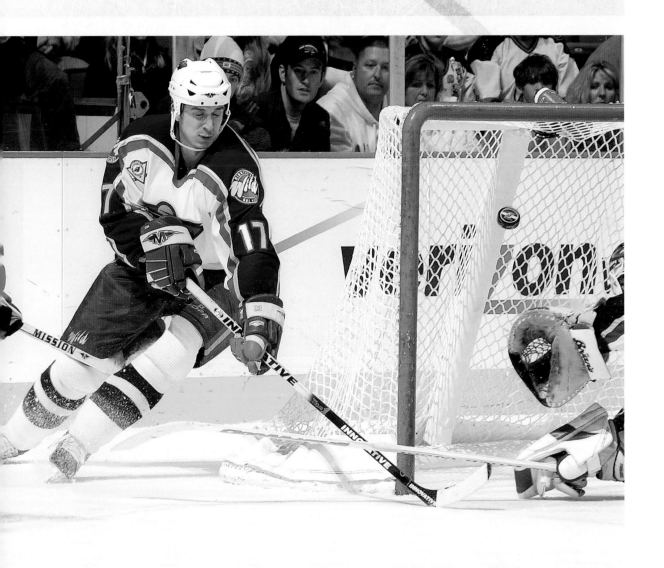

Although he started his Wild career as a relative unknown, Filip Kuba quietly became one of the NHL's top defensemen and a 2004 All-Star.

when the Wild returned to the Xcel Energy Center on October 5, 2005, the fans were back in full force.

Those fans cheered on the efforts of some new players wearing Wild red and green. Imposing (6-foot-7 and 260 pounds) wing Derek Boogaard, a reserved, bespectacled man away from the game, emerged as a fearless enforcer on the ice. Center Brian Rolston, who had been signed by Minnesota as a free agent before the cancelled 2004–05 season, added a powerful slap shot and stout defense to the lineup. Wing Stephane Veilleux, defenseman Kurtis Foster, and goalie Josh Harding also played key roles that season. The Wild's fifth season ended with 38 wins, the second most in club history, but Minnesota again missed the postseason. "The season was a rollercoaster," said Gaborik. "Overall it wasn't bad, but we want to get to the playoffs. That's our goal, so we fell short."

"I tell players to never doubt your confidence and never doubt your shot, because the top scorers are like that."

MINNESOTA HEAD COACH JACQUES LEMAIRE

Land of Many Captains

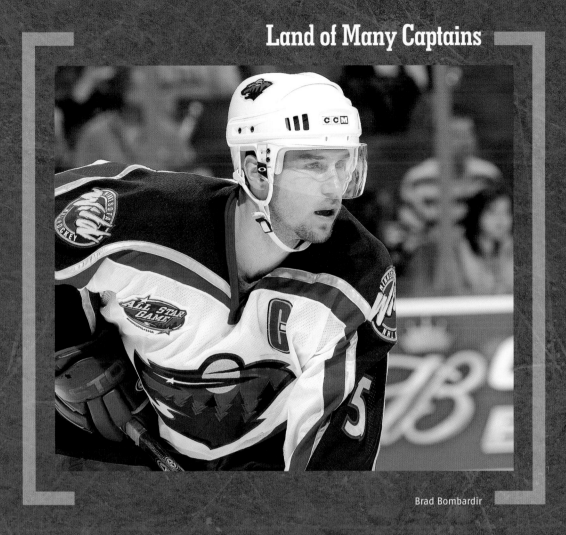

Brad Bombardir

THROUGHOUT THE WILD'S SHORT HISTORY, the team has rotated team captains every month. This policy is in contrast with most other NHL teams, which designate captains for full seasons. At the start of each month during the team's first seven seasons, Wild general manager Doug Risebrough, coach Jacques Lemaire, and the team's assistant coaches chose a player who exemplified great leadership and character qualities both in and out of his skates. Defenseman Sean O'Donnell was the first recipient of the honor in October 2000, while defenseman Brad Bombardir held the rank four out of the six months during the 2002–03 campaign. "You give the opportunity to different players to be proud of being on the team and the captain of that team," explained Lemaire. "If [a player has] the 'C,' and you don't feel that the player is as good or he's not as good as a leader, what are you going to do, take it off?" Wing Andrew Brunette, who wore the prestigious captain badge four times in three seasons, said it "made everyone feel like they were a leader." The franchise embraced the policy largely because the rotating captaincy de-emphasized individual stars and instead stressed team unity.

ON THE PROWL AGAIN

BEFORE THE START OF THE 2006–07 SEASON, the Wild added some new names to the lineup. They acquired Petteri Nummelin, a defenseman with surprising offensive talent, and Branko Radivojevic, a hard-charging wing. The franchise also made a big draft-day trade to pick up Los Angeles Kings winger Pavol Demitra, a dynamic playmaker who would partner well with fellow Slovakian Marian Gaborik. And finally, the Wild added some toughness by signing three free agents: wing (and Minnesota native) Mark Parrish and defensemen Kim Johnsson and Keith Carney.

Known for his goalie-fooling move called the "Shoulder Shake," Petteri Nummelin was one of the game's top scorers in overtime shootouts.

The scoring of center Mikko Koivu helped Minnesota start the season with a six-game winning streak. As the season unfolded, fans saw the Wild mature into a more confident and consistent club. The team put together another win streak in March, this time nine straight games—a franchise record. By the time the buzzer sounded on the final regular-season game, the Wild owned a 48–26–8 mark and had set a slew of team records, including goals (235) and shots (2,431) in a season. Minnesota then marched into the playoffs to face the Anaheim Ducks.

Anaheim captured the first three games, winning each by a single goal. Although the Wild roared back for a 4–1 victory in Game 4, the game was overshadowed by a violent incident late in the third period. As several players pushed and shoved, Ducks wing Brad May threw a punch that knocked Johnsson out of both the game and the series with a concussion. The blow

Filip Kuba DEFENSEMAN

Kuba enjoyed both hockey and soccer as a kid but decided to stick with hockey, a sport he watched his father and older brother play. It was a decision that proved to be a smart one. After Kuba spent two unremarkable seasons with the Florida Panthers, the new Wild franchise selected him in the 2000 NHL Expansion Draft. In five seasons, Kuba led the Minnesota team in average ice time—almost 24 minutes per game—and demonstrated some offensive skill by scoring 14 power-play goals. Always a player with great instincts, he also learned to use his big frame better to smother opponents.

WILD SEASONS: 2000–06
HEIGHT: 6-4
WEIGHT: 225

- 761 career shots on goal
- 81 power-play points (goals plus assists)
- member of the 2006 Czech Republic Olympic team
- 2004 All-Star

The sixth pick of the 2001 NHL Draft, multitalented center Mikko Koivu became a Minnesota star as he helped lead the Wild to the 2007 playoffs.

infuriated Coach Lemaire and Johnsson's teammates, and Boogaard spent the game's final minutes unsuccessfully looking to pick a fight with any Anaheim player. "Johnsson's not a fighter," Lemaire said. "If [May is] looking for someone, we've got one. His number is 24 [Boogaard], and he's the tallest."

Game 5 in Anaheim's Honda Center started with fireworks as well, as Boogaard and Ducks defenseman Chris Pronger tangled during warmups. Unfortunately, Minnesota was left even more frustrated by the game's end. Gaborik scored a short-handed goal in the second period, but that was all Minnesota could muster, losing the game and series 4–1. "If you're any type of athlete and you're satisfied with just making the playoffs, you're a bit of a loser," said Walz. "You play the game to win championships."

> "[Jacques Lemaire] basically took a slab of clay that was nothing and made me into a player that I can be proud of."
>
> MINNESOTA CENTER WES WALZ

The Wild bid farewell to one of their longtime stars after the season when they traded Manny Fernandez to Boston, but goalie Niklas Backstrom—who had played brilliantly when Fernandez went down with an injury the previous season—was ready to fill the void. As had become their habit, the Wild opened the 2007–08 season on a hot streak, winning their first five games, but they soon stumbled through a five-game losing streak as well. On December 1, the team suffered another key loss when Walz announced his

Minnesota Fight Song

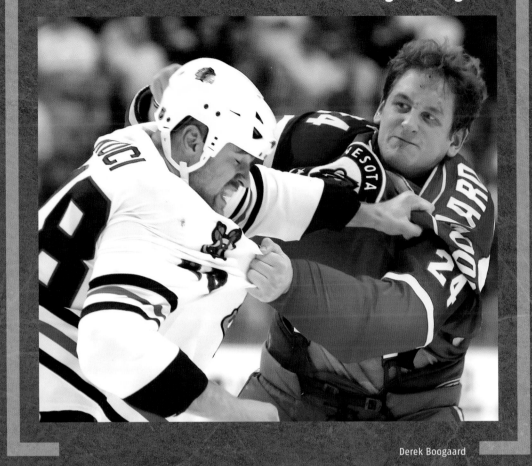

Derek Boogaard

ALTHOUGH MANY NHL CLUBS HAVE SPECIAL songs that are played after goals or victories, the Wild has its own very unique anthem. John Olson, the head of an advertising agency hired in 1998 to help create the Minnesota team's identity and marketing after NHL expansion was granted, wrote the anthem lyrics and music before players ever hit the ice for the first time. He created an energetic, Irish-sounding song focused on the most important part of the new franchise: the fans, or what Olson called "the spiritual owners of the team." Especially after the North Stars left town, Olson wanted to make sure that people knew one thing: Minnesota would not stand to lose another hockey team. The lyrics state, "The day they try to take this game / Is the day the gloves come off." The anthem is played—and featured on the scoreboard—at every Wild game at the Xcel Energy Center, during one of the between-period intermissions. Although Olson admitted that the song is intended to be humorous, "people understand that the meaning behind it is very serious." As the second stanza states, "The game's in our blood / And our blood's in the game."

retirement. The 37-year-old decided he could no longer play up to his own standards, and his retirement left Gaborik as the only original Wild player from 2000 still on the roster.

The first half of the season included more ups and downs, but win or lose, fan support for the Wild never wavered. Minnesota's passionate fan base earned national recognition in December 2007, when *Sports Illustrated* proclaimed St. Paul to be the new "Hockeytown U.S.A." (a tag that had long been applied to Detroit). In so honoring Minnesota and its capital, writer Michael Farber cited the fact that every home game in the Wild's history had been a sellout, and that some 7,500 fans remained on a waiting list for a chance to purchase season tickets. "This is a franchise respectful of the game, aware of its niche, and [most accommodating] in its treatment of fans," he noted.

Manny Fernandez GOALIE

Fernandez started his NHL career with Minnesota's former franchise, the Dallas Stars. He tended the nets for the Wild their first six seasons before being traded to the Boston Bruins in 2007. Fernandez had been plagued by inconsistent play in Dallas, but during his time with Minnesota, he improved his defense by switching from an almost stand-up style (one knee down, one up) to a "butterfly" style (dropping to knees) of goaltending. An energetic player with quick reflexes and a fiercely competitive streak, Fernandez seemed to have hockey in his blood, as he was the nephew of Wild coach Jacques Lemaire.

WILD SEASONS: 2000–07
HEIGHT: 6-0
WEIGHT: 207

- 14 career shutouts
- 2007 Jennings Award co-winner (fewest goals allowed in a season)
- career-high 30 wins in 2005–06
- team-record 113 wins

A quiet but determined player, Niklas Backstrom became the team's top netminder after a great 2006–07 season in which he built a 23–8–6 record.

By the midseason All-Star break, the Wild sat atop the Northwest Division with a 28–19–3 record. Besides the high-scoring Gaborik, top contributors included defenseman Brent Burns, versatile center Mikko Koivu, and slick-passing wing Pierre-Marc Bouchard. This core of young stars made a push for Minnesota's third postseason berth under the watch of proud new owner Craig Leipold, former owner of the Nashville Predators. "Throughout the entire league, when you look at a [team] that embodies everything that every franchise wants to be, this is the marquee franchise," said Leipold, who purchased the Wild in January 2008. "This is the new standard in the NHL."

Like a bear cub, the Minnesota Wild started out small in 2000 but have grown quickly and now have intentions of becoming a beast in the NHL. With proven coach Jacques Lemaire behind the bench, stars such as Marian Gaborik and Niklas Backstrom on the ice, and nearly 20,000 vocal fans in the stands for every home game, the Wild have good reason to believe that it is only a matter of time before the Stanley Cup is theirs. After all, hockey's greatest prize would only be a natural fit in Minnesota, the state of hockey, and St. Paul, Hockeytown U.S.A.

"There is a real attachment between these Wild players and their fan base. They're educated fans who love their hockey, and they have high expectations."

MINNESOTA SPORTSCASTER MARK ROSEN

WILD

Gaborik's Flurry

ON DECEMBER 26, 1996, DETROIT RED WINGS star center Sergei Fedorov scored an incredible five goals in a single game—a feat that went unmatched in the NHL for 11 years. The rare hat trick plus two didn't recur until Minnesota Wild star Marian Gaborik "lit the lamp" five times in one of the most memorable games in team history. On December 20, 2007, playing before a rocking Wild home crowd, Minnesota's speed demon shredded the New York Rangers' defense for five goals in a 6–3 Wild victory. The winger seemed to be everywhere on the ice, netting one goal in the first period, two in the second, and two in the third, ending the scoring explosion with a breathtaking breakaway goal. Gaborik even managed to notch an assist, and when the final buzzer sounded, he was carried off the ice by Wild defensemen Sean Hill and Keith Carney. Afterward, the shy star was humble about the accomplishment, letting his teammates do most of the talking. "It was pretty amazing," said wing Mark Parrish. "He was banking 'em in out of the air, scoring on breakaways, skating through everybody with it.... When a guy like that's feeling it, it gets pretty scary for the other team."

Marian Gaborik was the fastest and most explosive scorer in Wild history, netting many goals in highlight-reel fashion on breakaway opportunities.

Jacques Lemaire COACH

A native of Quebec, Canada, Lemaire was a standout center with a blistering slap shot for the Montreal Canadiens in the 1960s and '70s. After successful coaching stints with the Canadiens and the New Jersey Devils, he became the coach of the expansion Wild in 2000. Lemaire instituted several unusual philosophies in Minnesota, such as mixing and matching lineups during games, employing stifling defensive strategies, and rotating team captains monthly. The stern but sharp-witted Lemaire brought vast experience to the Wild, being the first man in NHL history with 100 or more NHL playoff games as both a player and a head coach.

WILD SEASONS AS COACH: 2000–present
NHL COACHING RECORD: 456–353–158
2-TIME NHL COACH OF THE YEAR
HOCKEY HALL OF FAME INDUCTEE (1984)

WILD

INDEX

WILD